NEW YC

CHRISTMAS GUIDE

A Definitive Guide to a Memorable Christmas Adventure in New York City, USA.

BETTY R. CROSS

COPYRIGHT

TABLE OF CONTENTS

INTRODUCTION

The streets of New York City come alive with the glitter of a million lights during the Christmas season, and the air is filled with the merry sounds of carolers and laughing. Welcome to the Magic of Christmas in New York, the city that never sleeps and a time unlike any other. In this book, we'll take you on a tour of the magic and merriment that is a New York Christmas and give you insights, advice, and suggestions to help you have an absolutely unique experience.

About This Guide

This comprehensive travel guide will help you discover the wonder of Christmas in the heart of Manhattan and beyond. This guide is made to suit all your requirements and interests throughout this Christmas season, whether you're a first-time visitor or a seasoned New York aficionado.

Our goal is to provide you a thorough road plan for a pleasant vacation. We have carefully selected the finest of what New York has to offer for the holiday season, including famous attractions, little-known attractions, delicious restaurants, exciting cultural activities, and much more. You'll be able to create your own special New York Christmas journey with the knowledge and suggestions in this book.

Maximising This Guide

It's critical to understand how to use this book successfully if you want to get the most out of your New York Christmas vacation. Here is a quick explanation of how to use it:

Chapter Navigation: This guide is divided into sections, each of which focuses on a distinct element of your New York Christmas experience. The areas that doesn't interest you can be quickly skipped.

Attraction Highlights: This list includes suggestions for must-see landmarks, activities, and events. To make sure you don't miss out on the finest experiences, keep an eye out for these highlighted parts.

Practical Information: To assist you in smoothly planning your vacation, we've included some useful information and recommendations. These sections include helpful advice on a variety of topics, including lodging reservations, financial management, and using public transit.

Local Insights: We want you to have a true sense of the diversity and energy of the city of New York. Be on the lookout for local knowledge and advice that might point you in the direction of undiscovered attractions and genuine encounters.

Sample of Itineraries: Sample itineraries have been provided to help you plan and visualize your days so you can make the most of your time in the city.

Appendices: To help you with your planning, you'll find helpful links, a packing list, example itineraries, and a glossary of terminology related to New York Christmas after the book.

Tips for a Special New York Christmas

Many people's dreams of having a New York Christmas come true, but there is so much to see and do that it may sometimes be a little daunting. Here are some helpful hints to make sure your trip to New York City during the holidays is nothing short of magical:

Plan Ahead: Because New York is so busy during the holidays, you must make travel arrangements well in advance. To ensure you have the finest alternatives and prevent disappointments, make reservations for your lodging, flights, and tickets to popular attractions well in advance.

Dress Warmly: December in New York can be rather frigid. Be sure to dress in layers and don't forget your thick coat, gloves, and cap. To navigate the city streets, you must wear comfortable walking shoes.

Budget Wisely: Holiday meals and shopping might tempt you to overpay. For your vacation, establish a budget and stick to it. To conserve money and yet have a good time over the holidays, look for free or inexpensive events and investigate eating alternatives that are within your budget.

Use Public Transit: New York City has a robust and effective public transit system. Use the buses and subways to navigate the city and save time and money. Think about getting a MetroCard for convenient access.

Arrive Early: Arrive early since ice skating rinks and the Rockefeller Center Christmas Tree may get busy very fast. You can avoid the crowds and experience these activities with reduced wait times by getting there early in the day.

Embrace Local Traditions: New York has its own special holiday customs, including viewing the Rockettes at Radio City Music Hall or enjoying a traditional cream cheese-topped bagel. Accept these customs to fully ingratiate yourself with the community.

Security Awareness: In busy situations, stay mindful of your surroundings and watch out for your possessions. Even though New York is typically secure, it is always a good idea to be on the lookout, particularly in densely populated locations.

You're well on your way to making priceless memories during your New York Christmas Odyssey with these suggestions and this manual in hand. Consequently, let's plunge in and explore the enchanted world of a New York Christmas as a group.

PLANNING YOUR TRIP

Planning your holiday journey in New York is a fun task that has the promise of wonderful moments and memorable encounters. This chapter serves as your indispensable starting point and ensures that your vacation will be well-planned, entertaining, and memorable. Everything will be covered, from picking the ideal time to go to practical advice for preparing for a winter trip.

Choosing the Best Time to Visit

The Christmas season in New York City begins in late November and lasts until early January. The whole period is beautiful, however, there are certainly important factors to take into account while deciding when to visit:

Thanksgiving Weekend: Schedule your vacation for late November if you're eager to see the splendor of the Macy's Thanksgiving Day Parade. Booking your rooms well in advance is advised since this weekend can be packed.

Early December: For a more sedate and cost-effective experience, the first two weeks of December are great. Even without the busiest times, you may still enjoy the winter markets, ice skating, and seasonal decorations.

Mid-December to Christmas: With its busy streets, sparkling lights, and festive mood, this time frame is the definition of a New York Christmas. It's ideal if you want to really enjoy the Christmas season, but be ready for more crowds.

Post-Christmas to New Year's: throngs tend to drop out after Christmas Day, giving it a perfect time to explore without the throngs. The renowned Times Square Ball Drop is another option for bringing in the new year.

Early January: This is the ideal time to go if you want a more sedate and economical experience. While some Christmas decorations are still up, the city settles back into its routine, letting you take in the sights with fewer visitors.

Budgeting for Your Christmas Adventure

Even while a New York Christmas might be wonderful and pricey, it can also be. Making a budget is an essential step to guaranteeing you have a good time without going overboard with your spending. How to begin going is as follows:

Set a Total Budget: Decide how much you're willing to spend on all aspects of your vacation, including lodging, food, activities, and mementos.

Break Down Expenses: Spending should be broken down into other areas, such as lodging, travel, meals, activities, and shopping. You may more effectively distribute finances with the aid of this breakdown.

Research Costs: Cost research is important. Find out in advance how much lodging, admission to attractions, and meals will cost. Look for unique holiday packages, bargains, and savings.

Consider Free & Low-Cost Activities: New York provides a variety of free and low-cost holiday activities, such as taking in the city's Christmas lights or visiting local markets. To save money, include them in your schedule.

Track Your Spending: Use a spreadsheet or budgeting program to keep tabs on your outing's costs. This will enable you to stick to your spending plan and make any modifications.

Emergency Fund: Include an emergency reserve in your spending plan to pay for unforeseen costs or crises. Having some extra money on hand is usually a good idea.

Booking Accommodation in New York

Making the appropriate lodging selections is an important part of organizing your New York Christmas journey. The following advice will help you locate the ideal lodging:

Location is Important: If you want to be close to holiday activities, consider staying in

Manhattan, particularly in areas like Midtown, Times Square, or the Upper West Side. There are other excellent alternatives in Brooklyn and Queens, each with a distinct flavor.

Book in Advance: To get the greatest discounts and availability, you must reserve your lodging well in advance since New York is a popular vacation destination.

Budget vs. Luxury: Choose between cheap and expensive accommodations. Luxury hotels, as well as inexpensive hostels and vacation rentals, are all available in New York. Choose depending on your tastes and budget.

Check Reviews: To get information from other travelers, read reviews on websites like TripAdvisor or Booking.com Take note of remarks made on location, cleanliness, and customer service.

Consider Amenities: Consider the facilities that are important to you. Some hotels include free breakfast, exercise facilities, or even on-site vacation activities.

Accessibility: To make it simpler to explore the city, make sure your lodging is conveniently close to transit hubs.

Transportation Options

Traveling through New York at this time of year may be an experience in and of itself. Consider the following possibilities for transportation:

Subway: One of the most effective methods to get about the city is the New York City subway system. Get a MetroCard to get quick access to bus and subway services.

Bus: Another dependable means of transportation is the bus, particularly if the subway does not immediately go to your location.

Walking: New York is a walking city, so taking a stroll around the streets to take in the Christmas spirit is a great idea. For winter strolls, make sure you're dressed warmly.

Taxis & Rideshares: Taxis and ridesharing services like Uber and Lyft are widely accessible but bear in mind that during busy holiday hours, traffic might be backed up.

Biking: If you're an adventurous visitor, you may want to check out the city's bike lanes. Simply use caution over the winter.

Ferries: Ferries are the best option if you want to go to places like the Statue of Liberty or Ellis Island.

Airport Transportation: Transportation from the airport to your lodging should be scheduled in advance. Taxis, rideshares, and airport shuttles are available options.

Packing Tips for a Winter Visit

To keep warm, cozy, and fashionable on a winter trip to New York, you must pack with care. What to include on your packing list is as follows:

Warm Clothing: To remain warm in the frigid weather, bring a thick coat, gloves, a scarf, and a hat. The trick is to layer so you may modify your attire as necessary.

Bring comfortable, waterproof boots so you can navigate the slippery streets. If you want to visit ice rinks, think about bringing along an additional pair of socks.

Electronics and Chargers: To capture the enchantment of the holidays and maintain connectivity, don't forget your camera, smartphone, and chargers.

Travel Adapter: Keep in mind to take a travel adapter for your electrical gadgets if you're going abroad.

Travel Documents: Store your passport, ID, trip insurance, and itinerary in a safe location that is also conveniently accessible.

Cash and Cards: Carry a combination of credit cards and cash, and tell your bank about your vacation intentions to prevent any problems with card use.

Medications & Toiletries: Bring any essential prescription drugs along with amenities like travel-sized shampoo, toothpaste, and a toothbrush.

Reusable Water Bottle: Bring a reusable water bottle that you may fill up as needed to stay hydrated during the day.

Backpack or Daypack: If you want to shop or visit the city for a long amount of time, a compact backpack or daypack will be useful for transporting necessities.

Umbrella: In the event of unforeseen rain or snow, a small, portable umbrella may be quite helpful.

You'll be well-prepared to start your New York Christmas experience if you use this preparatory advice. Careful planning and preparation are essential to a successful vacation, enabling you to fully enjoy the city's magic throughout the holiday season. You're prepared to experience the marvels of New York over Christmas now that your arrangements are in order.

MUST-SEE CHRISTMAS ATTRACTIONS

During the holiday season, New York City changes into a winter wonderland and offers a wide range of wonderful attractions that embody the spirit of Christmas. This chapter will examine the Christmas attractions that are a must-see in New York City and capture the spirit of the holiday. Each encounter is a tribute to the city's holiday spirit, from the recognizable Rockefeller Center Christmas Tree to the sparkling lights all over the place.

Rockefeller Center & the Iconic Christmas Tree

At the center of New York's holiday celebrations, Rockefeller Center is a sight to see. Here are some reasons to visit it:

The Christmas Tree: The tall Christmas tree, which is decorated with tens of thousands of sparkling lights and a glittering Swarovski crystal star, serves as the focal point of

Rockefeller Center. The star-studded lighting ceremony, which usually takes place in early December, is a popular tradition.

Ice Skating: Lace up your skates and skate over the renowned Rink at Rockefeller Center under the tree. A traditional New York Christmas tradition is ice skating under the tall tree.

Decorations & Atmosphere: The whole plaza is decked up in holiday decorations, including huge ornaments and a stunning display of angels. Christmas music and the aroma of roasted chestnuts permeate the air.

Ice Skating at Wollman Rink

Go to Wollman Rink in Central Park for other ice-skating possibilities. This charming rink provides a peaceful location among the winter wonder of the park. What makes it unique is as follows:

Central Park Backdrop: Ice skating in this location enables you to take in the wintertime elegance of Central Park. It's a peaceful retreat because of the woods around it and the distant city skyline.

Twinkling Lights: During nighttime sessions, the rink is exquisitely lighted with glittering lights, providing a romantic atmosphere.

Hot Chocolate: Warm up with a cup of hot chocolate at the rinkside café after a spin on the ice.

Window Displays on Fifth Avenue

Some of the most prominent department shops in the world have extravagant Christmas window displays on Fifth Avenue. Here's what to anticipate:

Saks Fifth Avenue: The elaborate light displays and yearly-changing themes in Saks' windows are a visual extravaganza. Their exhibitions' public debut is much awaited.

Macy's Herald Square: Intricate window displays may be seen at Macy's Herald Square, which often coordinates them with their

Thanksgiving Day Parade. Don't forget to check out the Santaland Christmas area inside.

Bergdorf Goodman: Known for its imaginative window displays, Bergdorf Goodman creates a one-of-a-kind visual experience with its windows that blend fashion with fantasy.

Tiffany & Co.: Known for its stunning simplicity, Tiffany's displays, with their recognizable blue boxes, evoke the spirit of the festive season.

Holiday Markets and Shopping

The Christmas markets in New York City are a veritable gold mine of unusual presents, handmade goods, and delectable delights. Some of the top markets to check out are listed below:

Union Square Holiday Market: This market has over 100 craftsmen and exhibitors who sell a variety of gifts, including gourmet cuisine and handmade jewelry.

Bryant Park Winter Village: Bryant Park Winter Village is a picturesque community with an ice skating rink, attractive stores in glass kiosks, and a magical ambiance. It is located behind the New York Public Library.

Columbus Circle Holiday Market: At the entrance to Central Park, there is a market called Columbus Circle Holiday Market that has a carefully picked assortment of presents, jewelry, and home products.

Grand Central Holiday Fair: Located within the famous Grand Central Terminal, this market is ideal for last-minute gift-buying since it offers distinctive items made by regional craftsmen.

Visiting Santa Claus in New York

Santa Claus visits are a treasured ritual for families and young at heart. Where in the city can you locate Santa?

Macy's Santaland: Santa himself is ready to hear your Christmas wishes at Macy's

Santaland, which is a winter paradise within the Herald Square Macy's.

Brookfield Place: In Lower Manhattan, Santa Claus opens his shop at Brookfield Place, where you may see him and take special pictures.

Bronx Zoo Holiday Lights: The Bronx Zoo's Holiday Lights program combines a trip to observe animals with a chance to meet Santa Claus in a festive environment.

Spectacular Christmas Show at Radio City Music Hall

For decades, audiences have been enchanted by the glittering, high-octane Radio City Christmas Spectacular. What makes it a must-see is as follows:

The Rockettes: The world-famous Rockettes, who are renowned for their precise dance routines, sparkly outfits, and signature high kicks, appear in the production.

Live Music: Hear traditional Christmas songs and carols performed live, as well as a magnificent organ performance.

Stunning Visuals: The program uses both modern technology and classic components to produce a visual spectacle that perfectly captures the spirit of Christmas.

The Nutcracker Ballet at Lincoln Center

The Nutcracker ballet's captivating story may be seen at the Lincoln Center. What makes it a cherished holiday custom is as follows:

World-Class Performers: This show has top-notch dancers, gorgeous costumes, and Tchaikovsky's ageless music.

Magical Set Design: The ballet's elaborate set design and choreography will transport you to the enchanted realm of Clara and her Nutcracker Prince.

Family-Friendly: This performance is great for introducing kids to the arts since it is suitable for audiences of all ages.

Holiday Lights and Decorations Across the City

New York City's streets, parks, and monuments are all decked up for the holidays. Here are a few of the more spectacular performances:

Dyker Heights: Visit the Dyker Heights neighborhood in Brooklyn, where many go all out with lavish Christmas light displays on their houses.

The Plaza Hotel: The Plaza Hotel's facade is decorated with classy Christmas lights, which gives the area surrounding this famous hotel a festive feel.

DUMBO's Manhattan Bridge Archway: An enormous, interactive light display can be seen near the Manhattan Bridge Archway in DUMBO, Brooklyn, which makes it the ideal location for Christmas portraits.

Saks Fifth Avenue Light Show: Throughout the evening, Saks turns its outside into a beautiful light display that mesmerizes onlookers.

Holiday Train Show at the New York Botanical Garden: At the New York Botanical Garden's Holiday Train Show, see model trains rumbling through a scaled-down version of New York City decorated for the season with twinkling lights.

The Christmas attractions in New York City are proof that the city can provide magical moments over the holiday season. Every encounter contributes to the tapestry of Christmas memories in the Big Apple, from well-known customs like the Rockefeller Center Christmas Tree and the Radio City Christmas Spectacular to the wonder of seasonal lights and shopping. Embrace the holiday mood and make the most of these New York Christmas must-see sites.

DINING & CULINARY DELIGHTS

Discovering New York City's culinary delights over the holidays is an adventure that will tantalize your taste buds and leave you with priceless memories. We'll delve into the culinary delights that are in store for you in this chapter, from traditional holiday feasts to decadent hot chocolate, eating with stunning vistas, and the merry vibe of food markets and festivals.

Traditional Holiday Meals in New York

Savoring a classic holiday feast is one of the most iconic aspects of a New York Christmas. Reservations are strongly advised at the city's many restaurants, which all provide special holiday menus. Here are some well-known foods and restaurants to think about:

Roast Turkey: Enjoy a traditional roast turkey meal with all the fixings, such as stuffing, cranberry sauce, and gravy. This classic dish is a staple of the holiday menus at many eateries.

Christmas Ham: If ham is more your style, you may get delicious glazed ham dishes, which are a Christmas staple.

Christmas Geese: Christmas geese is a rich and savory meal that some restaurants offer on their menus for diners with a more adventurous taste.

Feast of the Seven Fishes: Enjoy the Feast of the Seven Fishes, a seafood-heavy supper generally eaten on Christmas Eve, and embrace an Italian-American tradition.

Holiday Desserts: Save space for dessert! Try traditional desserts like fruitcake, gingerbread cookies, or a warm piece of pecan pie.

Reservations: Make reservations well in advance since popular holiday restaurants tend to book up fast. Holiday meals are available in well-known eateries like Balthazar, Gramercy Tavern, and Tavern on the Green.

Hot Chocolate & Holiday Treats

Warm-up and satisfy your sweet craving with delicious hot chocolate and seasonal sweets from New York. Where to locate the finest is as follows:

City's Best Hot Chocolate: For rich, creamy hot chocolate topped with marshmallows or whipped cream, go to famous locations like City Bakery or Serendipity 3.

Artisanal Bakeries: Explore specialty bakeries like Magnolia Bakery for its renowned banana pudding and festive cupcakes, or Levain Bakery for their giant cookies.

Candy Shops: For holiday-themed goodies, candy canes, and distinctive confections, head to Dylan's Candy Bar, a famous candy shop.

Holiday Markets: If you want to try a variety of savory and sweet delights, don't miss the holiday markets. You must go to the Bryant

Park Winter Village and the Union Square Holiday Market.

Dining with a View

With so many beautiful vistas in New York City, eating and taking in the season can be a magical experience. Here are a few possibilities:

The View Restaurant & Lounge: A rotating restaurant and lounge in Times Square that serves meals with sweeping views of the metropolitan skyline.

Top of the Rock: Eat at The Sea Grill or Bar SixtyFive in the Rainbow Room at the top of Rockefeller Center. These locations provide breathtaking views of the famous Christmas tree of the city.

One Dine: One Dine is a restaurant that provides breathtaking views of Manhattan and the harbor as you enjoy a special meal. It is located at One World Observatory in the Freedom Tower.

River Café: The River Café offers a sophisticated dining experience with beautiful views of the Manhattan skyline while being tucked under the Brooklyn Bridge.

Exploring Food Markets & Festivals

New York City comes alive throughout the Christmas season with food markets and festivities that honor various culinary traditions. How to maximize this festive food scenario is as follows:

Union Square Holiday Market: Holiday food vendors selling gourmet chocolates, artisanal cheeses, exotic cuisine, and more may be found at the Union Square Market.

Bryant Park Winter Village: Discover more than 150 seasonal shops and food stalls at Bryant Park Winter Village, where you can get anything from toasty pretzels to upscale macaroni and cheese.

Holiday Food Festivals: Keep an eye out for specific food festivals and events for the holidays where you may taste cuisine from all over the globe and enjoy the flavors of the time of year.

Food Truck Delights: Don't forget to sample some of New York's renowned food trucks, which serve up anything from exquisite tacos to delectable sandwiches.

Be ready to go on a gastronomic adventure that represents the city's vast ethnic variety as you discover the culinary wonders of New York during the Christmas season. Your Christmas vacation will be enhanced by New York's food scene, which offers everything from traditional holiday fare to sweet pleasures and restaurants with stunning vistas. So, relish each mouthful and let your taste senses experience the city's Christmas enthusiasm.

EXPERIENCE NEW YORK'S CHRISTMAS SPIRIT

During the holiday season, New York City comes to life with the Christmas spirit, delivering a wide range of touching and joyful experiences that capture the genuine spirit of the occasion. In this chapter, we'll look at the several ways you may get into the Christmas spirit in New York, from carol singing and choir performances to holiday parades and festivals, as well as the chance to volunteer and take in local churches' religious events.

Caroling & Choir Performances

St. Patrick's Cathedral: A spectacular Neo-Gothic masterpiece that serves as a place of prayer and meditation. It is situated on Fifth Avenue. The cathedral presents several joyous concerts and caroling occasions during the Christmas season that include famous choirs and musicians. Attending one of these events is a fantastic chance to take in the breathtaking scenery and beauty of Christmas music.

The Cloisters: The Cloisters, a division of the Metropolitan Museum of Art devoted to medieval European art, offer a distinctive Christmas experience. The museum often presents holiday concerts and shows that immerse you in the sounds of the Renaissance and the Middle Ages. The serene gardens and historic buildings provide an alluring setting for these performances.

Washington Square Park: Join in on the holiday cheer at Washington Square Park, where neighborhood ensembles and musicians often assemble to perform carols. The park's famous arch makes for a gorgeous backdrop, and you may participate in the singing or just enjoy the season.

Public Caroling Events: Watch out for public carol-singing activities taking place all across the city. Caroling events are often organized by organizations and community groups in parks, squares, and other public areas, and everyone is welcome to attend.

Holiday Parades and Festivals

Macy's Thanksgiving Day Parade: The Macy's Thanksgiving Day Parade ushers in the holiday season with a bang, even though it doesn't take place in December per se. This festival is a must-see because of the spectacular floats, enormous balloons, marching bands, and performances by prominent performers. To have a good viewing location along the parade route, get there early.

Holiday Window Unveilings: Many of the shops on Fifth Avenue, including Macy's and Saks Fifth Avenue, put on lavish window unveiling celebrations. These events, which often include live shows, music, and celebrities, serve as the official unveiling of their Christmas window displays.

Hanukkah Celebrations: During the holiday season, New York City honors its many different cultures. Watch for Hanukkah events, such as the lighting of menorahs in open areas like Central Park and Brooklyn's Grand Army Plaza, which will include the biggest menorah in the world.

New Year's Eve in Times Square: Even though the Times Square Ball Drop on New Year's Eve is not officially a Christmas event, seeing it still is an exhilarating experience. Join the international partygoers as they ring in the new year in a sea of sparklers and confetti.

Volunteering & Giving Back

Consider volunteering with groups like New York Cares, which provides several opportunities all year long, including unique projects during the Christmas season. You may take part in projects like preparing meals at soup kitchens, wrapping presents for children in need, and more.

Food Banks and Shelters: During the holidays, several food banks and shelters in the city value volunteers. You may assist in feeding the hungry, serving meals, or making other significant contributions to aid people in need.

Toy Drives: To make sure that every kid gets a present for the holidays, several toy drives and gift-giving initiatives are held. Participate by providing toys or offering to assist with present distribution to households.

Holiday Giving Trees: Several charities put up Giving Trees where you may choose a tag that represents a gift request from a kid or family in need. Purchase the specified gift and return it to the organization so that it may be given out.

Homeless Outreach: Consider volunteering with groups that concentrate on helping the homeless. You may assist in providing warm clothes, blankets, and other supplies to those who are homeless.

Visiting Local Churches and Religious Celebrations

St. John the Divine: Visit the Cathedral of St. John the Divine, one of the biggest Gothic churches in the world, at St. John the Divine. The cathedral organizes several special services and performances that commemorate the birth of Christ throughout the Christmas season. There is a spiritual feeling brought about by the magnificent architecture and religious music.

St. Thomas Church Fifth Avenue: Several Advent and Christmas performances are held at St. Thomas Church Fifth Avenue, which is well-known for its lovely music program. The church is the ideal location to fully immerse oneself in the Christmas religious traditions thanks to its gorgeous decor and renowned choir.

Midnight Mass: For many people, it is a special custom to attend Midnight Mass on Christmas Eve. Midnight Mass services are offered by several churches across the city, including St. Patrick's Cathedral and Trinity Church, and are open to guests.

Religious Processions: During the Christmas season, several localities, especially those with strong cultural links, hold religious processions. For instance, a procession is held in East Harlem to commemorate the Feast of Our Lady of Guadalupe.

Interfaith Services: Attend interfaith services and events that bring people of different faiths together to celebrate the message of harmony and peace over the holidays to learn more about the city's unique religious landscape.

Embracing the pleasure, kindness, and giving that characterize the holiday season is key to experiencing the Christmas spirit in New York. You'll discover that the city's holiday spirit is contagious and will leave you with treasured memories of a New York Christmas full of love and goodwill, whether you choose to participate in caroling, go to holiday parades and festivals, volunteer to help the community or take part in religious celebrations.

EXPLORING THE BOROUGHS

The boroughs of New York City each provide their own distinctive brand of Christmas charm and festivities, even though Manhattan often commands attention throughout the holiday season. The holiday offerings in Brooklyn, Queens, and the Bronx, as well as the unique festivities on Staten Island, will be covered in this chapter. Beyond Manhattan's well-known tourist sites, these boroughs highlight their cultural variety by offering a diverse tapestry of vacation experiences.

Brooklyn's Holiday Charm

Brooklyn comes alive with Christmas splendor throughout the winter thanks to its distinctive neighborhoods and creative energy. The following highlights:

Dyker Heights Christmas Lights: The Brooklyn neighborhood of Dyker Heights is well known for its extravagant Christmas light displays. In one area, some houses go all out with extravagant decorations, transforming whole blocks into luminous wonderlands. Observing these magnificent displays during nighttime strolls or guided excursions around Dyker Heights has become a local custom.

Brooklyn Botanic Garden: During the Christmas season, the Brooklyn Botanic Garden holds its annual Glow event. The garden's bright winter sceneries, which include tens of thousands of lights, merry music, and warming stations for hot chocolate and marshmallow toasting, are open for visitors to meander around.

Barclays Center: The Barclays Center often presents unique holiday concerts and events with prominent musicians and artists. To determine whether your visit conflicts with a holiday show or performance, check the event calendar.

Neighborhood Markets: Williamsburg and DUMBO are just two of Brooklyn's many Christmas markets. These markets provide great locations for Christmas shopping because they provide distinctive gifts, artisanal cuisine, and locally made items.

Brooklyn Brewery: At the Brooklyn Brewery, warm up with a seasonal artisan beer. Numerous neighborhood brewers produce unique Christmas beers that perfectly capture the essence of the season.

Queens: A Diverse Christmas Experience

One of the most ethnically diverse counties in the US, Queens, provides a distinctive fusion of seasonal customs from across the globe. What you may anticipate is as follows:

Queens Botanical Garden: Winter Wonderland is an annual event that is held at the Queens Botanical Garden. While taking in live performances, Christmas crafts, and seasonal fare, visitors may explore the garden's dazzling holiday lights and decorations.

Jackson Heights: Known for its cultural richness, Jackson Heights is home to many different ethnic groups, each of which has its own special style of celebrating the holidays. Explore the area to see colorful exhibits, marketplaces, and special events that highlight a variety of customs.

Holiday Lights in the Gardens: Visit the Queens County Farm Museum for their annual Holiday Lights in the Garden celebration. For guests of all ages, the farm is decorated with hundreds of dazzling lights, which creates a beautiful environment.

Greek Orthodox Christmas: Astoria, which has a sizable Greek community, is a great place to experience a Greek Orthodox Christmas. Attend the joyous church services and indulge in baklava and pastitsio, two classic Greek holiday foods.

Flushing: The holidays bring out the best in Flushing's ethnic variety, with festivities from all walks of life. Discover the neighborhood's varied culinary scene, where you can savor original cuisines from across the world, including Latin American and Asian food.

The Bronx and Staten Island Celebrations

Even while Staten Island and The Bronx are less popular with visitors over the holidays, they nonetheless provide several festive activities:

The Bronx:

Bronx Zoo Holiday Lights: During this annual event, the zoo is transformed into a winter paradise. Along with other things, it has lit animal sculptures, eye-catching light shows, and ice carving demonstrations. A wonderful Christmas excursion for the whole family.

New York Botanical Garden: A much-loved yearly event is the Holiday Train Show in the Bronx's New York Botanical Garden. In tiny versions of famous New York City buildings, model trains go through beautiful botanical gardens that are decked up for the holidays.

Arthur Avenue: The Bronx neighborhood of Arthur Avenue, sometimes referred to as the "Real Little Italy," is a wonderful site to enjoy Italian holiday customs. Try Christmas goodies like panettone and cannoli at genuine Italian bakeries, stores, and restaurants.

Staten Island:

Staten Island Zoo Lights: An exciting Christmas event that includes dazzling light displays, carolers, and even the opportunity to see Santa Claus. It is held at the Staten Island Zoo. Families will have a fantastic time.

St. George Theatre: The historic St. George Theatre on Staten Island often holds Christmas shows, concerts, and screenings of vintage holiday movies. For activities during your stay with a festive theme, see their calendar.

Staten Island Ferry: For a distinctive perspective of the city's Christmas lighting, take a trip on the Staten Island Ferry. The Statue of Liberty, Ellis Island, and the Manhattan skyline—all beautifully lit for the holiday season—can be seen from the ship.

Conference House Park: Staten Island's Conference House Park is well-known for its stunning winter decorations and light shows.

It's a tranquil location to soak up the festive spirit and take a leisurely evening walk.

During the Christmas season, each of New York City's boroughs delivers a unique and varied experience. You'll find that the spirit of Christmas in New York transcends Manhattan's borders, whether you're taking in the opulence of Brooklyn's Dyker Heights, Queens' embrace of cultural variety, the Bronx's natural charms, or Staten Island's allure. To fully immerse yourself in the distinctive customs and joyous festivities that make the city's Christmas season so remarkable, see these boroughs.

OFF-THE-BEATEN-PATH ADVENTURES

New York City offers a world of off-the-beaten-path activities that expose a distinct side of the Christmas season beyond the sparkling lights and busy crowds of Manhattan's major holiday attractions. In this chapter, we'll go on unusual holiday excursions, get lost in Christmas-themed escape rooms, and learn about hidden jewels and neighborhood favorites that offer a more personal and unusual glimpse into New York's holiday spirit.

Unique Holiday Tours

Holiday Lights and Movie Sites Tour: Take a Holiday Lights and Movie Sites Tour for a truly cinematic holiday experience of the city. You'll see the dazzling holiday displays and decorations that have graced the silver screen along the way on this guided tour, which takes you through famous film locations featured in beloved holiday classics like "Home Alone 2," "Elf," and "Miracle on 34th Street."

Gingerbread House Workshops: Release your inner architect and enjoy the creative joy of making gingerbread buildings. You may create your own gingerbread masterpiece by designing, decorating, and assembling it at Gingerbread House Workshops held at various locations across the city. It's a pleasant and heartfelt approach to get into the Christmas mood that's ideal for groups of friends, families, or lone travelers.

Holiday Markets Shopping Tour: The city's holiday markets are a veritable gold mine of unusual presents and delicious food. Join a local expert who will accompany you through the busy booths on a Holiday Markets Shopping Tour. You'll come across one-of-a-kind gifts, artisanal cuisine, and hidden jewels while strolling around these quaint markets and soaking up the festive mood.

Ghost of Christmas Past Tour: Take a tour of the Ghost of Christmas history to learn more about the fascinating history of Christmas in New York. These historical excursions, conducted by professional guides, take you back in time while illuminating the city's festive customs and their development through time. You'll tour historical locations, hear enthralling tales, and discover the genesis of treasured traditions, providing a unique and instructive perspective on the time of year.

Christmas-Themed Escape Rooms

The Polar Express: Enter the magical world of "The Polar Express" in an escape room with a holiday theme. You may go on a beautiful trip with Santa Claus and his team in these interactive activities to get ready for Christmas. To guarantee a great Christmas season, work with your team to solve puzzles, interpret riddles, and more. It's an adventure that combines an imaginative storyline with exhilarating challenges, making it ideal for both families and puzzle fans.

A Christmas Carol: In an escape room based on the timeless tale by Charles Dickens, "A Christmas Carol," take a trip through its pages. To alter Ebenezer Scrooge's life, you and your team will follow in his footsteps by traveling through scenarios from the story. The festive joy and the spirit of redemption are well captured in this unique encounter.

The Nutcracker Mystery: In an escape room with a "The Nutcracker" theme, you may enter the enchanted world of the ballet and attempt to solve the mystery of the missing Nutcracker. You'll get engrossed in the colorful and enchanting world of this well-known Christmas tale as you figure out clues and solve riddles. It's an adventure that mixes imagination with a winter wonderland for a magical memory.

Santa's Workshop: In this Christmas-themed escape room, you'll be tasked with assisting Santa's diligent elves in finishing up their preparations for the season. Family-friendly puzzles, surprises, and a hint of winter wonderland abound in this journey. It's the ideal way to experience the beauty of the season with close friends and family.

Hidden Gems and Local Favorites

The Cloisters: The Cloisters, a hidden jewel in Upper Manhattan's Fort Tryon Park, provides a tranquil haven from the city's festive commotion. It is a division of the Metropolitan Museum of Art that focuses on the art and architecture of medieval Europe. The Cloisters' magnificently designed grounds are lit up for the holidays, resulting in a serene and entrancing ambiance. Examine the lit architecture as you stroll around the museum's medieval galleries and consider the actual meaning of the holiday season.

Green-Wood Cemetery: An intriguing location to visit during the holidays. It is unconventional but enthralling. It is located in Brooklyn. Annual Christmas performances are held in the cemetery's old chapel, filling the air with festive tunes. Wreaths and other seasonal accents have been placed around the cemetery's grounds, making it a peaceful and contemplative place to walk through and escape the Christmas hustle.

Le Parker Meridien's Holiday Burger: The hotel at Le Parker Meridien has a mouthwatering secret for food connoisseurs. During the holidays, Burger Business, the hotel's secret burger business, offers a unique seasonal burger. Only those in the know may get their hands on this delectable jewel, known as an off-menu dish. It's a pleasant and decadent Christmas treat that brings together the excitement of exploration and the pleasure of appreciating distinctive tastes.

DUMBO's Art Galleries: The Brooklyn neighborhood of DUMBO (Down Under the Manhattan Bridge Overpass) is a thriving center for creative expression. Visit the local painters' studios and galleries to see their creations. Many of these galleries hold special exhibits and activities around the holidays that honor the spirit of the time via works of art. It's a chance to take in the distinctive ambiance of DUMBO while appreciating local innovation.

Trinity Churchyard: Located in the center of the Financial District, Trinity Churchyard provides a tranquil respite from Lower Manhattan's busy streets. The graveyard is transformed into a peaceful Christmas sanctuary during the holidays with wreaths, glittering lights, and seasonal decorations. It's a tranquil place to take a break, meditate, and get away from the holiday hustle while appreciating the charm of a well-kept secret in the city.

Arthur Avenue: Arthur Avenue in the Bronx is sometimes referred to be New York City's "Real Little Italy" and is a gastronomic haven just waiting to be explored. The neighborhood comes to life during the holidays with spectacular decorations and the smells of authentic Italian holiday foods. Visit the genuine Italian bakeries, markets, and restaurants to savor seasonal treats like panettone and cannoli. In the middle of the Bronx, Arthur Avenue provides a true experience of Italian holiday customs.

You are invited to experience the off-the-beaten-path attractions that are part of the Christmas enchantment in New York City. Making gingerbread houses, solving mysteries in escape rooms with Christmas themes, learning about local favorites, or getting lost in the peace of hidden gems—all of these activities promise to reveal the city's distinctive and personal side during this most wonderful time of the year.

STAYING WARM & COZY

Finding methods to remain warm and comfy becomes crucial when the winter cold sets into New York City. We'll look at a variety of indoor activities, museums, warm pubs and lounges, and spa and wellness resorts in this chapter to help you have a pleasant and restorative trip in the city.

Indoor Activities & Museums

The Metropolitan Museum of Art: Sometimes referred to as "The Met," this Museum is a renowned museum with a vast collection of works of art that date back thousands of years. Explore its galleries for a day to see anything from contemporary works of art to treasures from ancient Egypt. The Met is the ideal place to get out of the cold and lose yourself in the world of art and culture.

The Museum of Modern Art (MoMA): Visit MoMA if you like modern art. This venerable museum exhibits a staggering selection of modern and contemporary works of art, including works by well-known creators like Picasso, Van Gogh, and Warhol. Its galleries are a pleasant and enlightening indoor experience to stroll around.

The American Museum of Natural History: Explore the fascinating realm of natural history at the famous American Museum of Natural History. Discover dinosaur fossils, elaborate dioramas, and cosmic displays. It's a fun indoor pastime for the whole family that teaches and entertains.

The Whitney Museum of American Art: The popular Meatpacking District is home to the Whitney Museum of American Art, which specializes in modern American art. It is a warm and interesting location to spend a cold day thanks to its thought-provoking displays and magnificent architecture.

The Museum of the Moving Image: The Museum of the Moving Image in Queens is a fascinating tour through the development of moving pictures for fans of movies and television. Discover recognizable props, engaging displays, and showings of old and modern movies.

The Morgan Library & Museum: This Library & Museum in Midtown Manhattan is a hidden treasure that houses an incredible collection of rare books, manuscripts, and works of art. Discover the ancient library, awe at beautiful manuscripts, and have a quiet hideaway from the chilly weather.

Cozy Bars and Lounges

The Campbell: The Campbell is a chic cocktail club with a classic feel, located within the famous Grand Central Terminal. It is a welcoming place to unwind and sip a drink because of its lengthy history and traditional drinks.

The Flatiron Room: A classy whiskey lounge in the Flatiron District, will jazz up your evening. In a warm and welcoming environment, sip on a variety of whiskeys while taking in live jazz performances.

The Dead Rabbit: The Dead Rabbit in the Financial District is a well-known Irish-American pub with a welcoming, friendly environment. In a welcoming pub-like environment, choose from a wide selection of inventive drinks, including their award-winning Irish coffee.

Bar Goto: Discover the allure of a Lower East Side cocktail bar with Japanese influences at Bar Goto. Bar Goto provides a comfortable haven with creative beverages and a tranquil atmosphere. Their specialty drinks, such as the Sakura Martini, are excellent and distinctive.

Employees Only: A speakeasy-style cocktail bar with a friendly environment that is located in the West Village. Employees Only is recognized for its artisan drinks. It's the perfect spot to relax and savor beverages that are skilfully crafted by knowledgeable bartenders.

Spa and Wellness Retreats

AIRE Ancient Baths: At AIRE Ancient Baths, you may escape to a peaceful sanctuary. This spa, which is housed in a renovated

Tribeca building, has thermal baths, massages, and relaxation zones that are reminiscent of old Roman baths. It offers a tranquil respite from the bustle of the metropolis.

Shibui Spa at The Greenwich Hotel: Shibui Spa is an urban haven located within The Greenwich Hotel in Tribeca. It has a pool, a Japanese-inspired decor, and a variety of spa services. Unwind in the lounge area lighted by lanterns after a massage or facial.

Great Jones Spa: A multi-level hideaway featuring water lounges, saunas, and a range of treatments. It is situated in the NoHo district. They have a thermal hot tub, a cold plunge pool, and a river-rock sauna in their renowned Water Lounge.

Cornelia Spa at The Surrey: Relax at Cornelia Spa, a chic haven on the Upper East Side, located in Surrey. The spa provides a variety of services in a calm and welcoming setting, including massages and facials.

The Mandarin Oriental Spa: This spa offers stunning views of the city from its vantage point high above Columbus Circle. Enjoy opulent services like their renowned Oriental Essence massage while unwinding in their tranquil relaxation area.

Russian & Turkish Baths: Visit the Russian & Turkish Baths in the East Village to enter a world of tradition and leisure. With saunas, steam rooms, cold pools, and other amenities, this historic spa provides a distinctive experience. It's a restorative getaway with a strong cultural component.

YeloSpa: With many sites across the city, YeloSpa provides a range of wellness treatments, such as reflexology, massages, and power naps. With a YeloNap, which offers a comfortable and private room to relax and regenerate, you can restore your energy.

You will appreciate the city's cultural treasures, unwind with a drink, or pamper yourself in a serene setting thanks to these indoor activities, toasty bars and lounges, and spa and health retreats. They provide your vacation in New York City with the ideal amount of warmth, comfort, and rest, guaranteeing that you have a wonderful time.

DAY TRIPS & NEARBY ATTRACTIONS

While New York City itself is home to a multitude of sights and activities, the neighboring areas also provide many options for day trips. Chapter 9 of "A New York Christmas Odyssey: Your Seasonal Travel Guide" discusses the exciting possibilities for seeing adjacent cities, taking part in outdoor activities, and enjoying peaceful retreats, whether you're looking for a change of scenery, an outdoor adventure, or a quiet break.

Visiting Nearby Cities & Towns

Hudson, New York: Less than two hours from Manhattan by car lies the quaint historic town of Hudson, New York, which is well-known for its attractive architecture, antique stores, and art galleries. Hudson becomes a winter paradise with seasonal decorations lining the streets over the holiday season. Visit the neighborhood shops to find one-of-a-kind Christmas presents, then have a hearty supper at one of the town's farm-to-table eateries.

Philadelphia, Pennsylvania: Philadelphia is just a short train journey away and provides an extensive historical experience, particularly during the holidays. Explore the Liberty Bell and Independence Hall, as well as the quaint lanes of Old City. Don't miss the yearly Christmas Village at LOVE Park where you can browse for presents from across the world and indulge in authentic German delights.

Princeton, New Jersey: Princeton is a gorgeous university town with a charming downtown area, and it is just one train ride from New York City. Visit the magnificent Princeton University campus, take in a show at the McCarter Theatre with a Christmas theme, and explore the Princeton Art Museum.

Outdoor Adventures

Bear Mountain State Park: A great day trip destination if you're looking for outdoor activity and spectacular natural beauty. This park, which is about an hour's drive from Manhattan, has hiking paths, breathtaking views of the Hudson River, and chances for winter activities like cross-country skiing and ice skating. The park is transformed into a merry paradise during the Christmas season with the yearly "Holiday Lights in Bloom" celebration.

Storm King Art Center: A distinctive outdoor sculpture park situated against the Hudson Highlands, only a short drive north of the city. Even though it's a well-liked attraction in the summer, going there in the winter offers a peaceful atmosphere since the sculptures are covered in snow. Holiday-themed activities and art displays are often held at the facility.

Mohonk Mountain House: A historic inn tucked away in the Shawangunk Mountains, situated in New Paltz, New York, roughly two hours drive from Manhattan. In this gorgeous alpine environment, you may engage in winter sports like ice skating, snowshoeing, and cuddling up by the fire. The resort is renowned for its charming Victorian style and friendly welcome.

Relaxing Getaways

The Catskills: The Catskill Mountains, which are a few hours' drive north of New York City, provide lovely getaways for those seeking a quiet getaway from the city. Several quaint inns and cottages provide the ideal environment for a relaxing vacation. Take picturesque roads, wander through quaint communities like Woodstock, and breathe in the clean mountain air.

The Hamptons: Although the Hamptons are often associated with the summer, they can provide a tranquil and opulent escape in the winter. Take advantage of spa services, exquisite cuisine, and deserted beaches. The Hamptons' many upscale boutique hotels and inns celebrate Christmas with unique events and packages.

The Hudson Valley: The Hudson Valley provides a wide variety of leisure possibilities with its undulating hills, wineries, and historic places. Visit vineyards for tastings, see opulent mansions like the Vanderbilt Mansion, and dine at quaint eateries serving farm-to-table fare.

The day trips and nearby attractions around New York City offer something for everyone, whether you're attracted to adjacent cities brimming with history and culture, crave outdoor experiences in picturesque landscapes, or looking for a calm respite from the holiday hustle and bustle. Make the most of your New York Christmas journey by visiting the surrounding areas, plan your day excursions in advance, and look for any holiday-themed events or attractions.

TIPS FOR A SMOOTH VISIT

To guarantee a smooth and joyful journey when you set off on your New York Christmas vacation, it's crucial to be well-prepared. In this section of "A New York Christmas Odyssey: Your Seasonal Travel Guide," we'll provide you helpful advice to make it easier for you to get about the city.

Weather Considerations

During the Christmas season, New York City enjoys a broad variety of weather conditions, from clear, bright days to frigid nights and the potential for snowfall. Observe the following weather-related advice:

Layer Up: Dress in layers so that you can adjust to the day's shifting temperatures. It is essential to wear a warm base layer, a sweater or fleece, and an insulated, waterproof upper layer. For warmth, remember to wear a thick winter coat, gloves, a hat, and a scarf.

Footwear: If you want to walk a lot or if there is snow or ice on the ground, you must wear comfortable, waterproof boots with adequate grip.

Check the Forecast: Keep abreast of the weather predictions while you are there. You may make better plans for your activities and wardrobe if you are aware of what to anticipate.

Alternatives Indoors: New York City has a wide variety of indoor attractions, including museums, theaters, and retail malls. Consider spending more time inside on chilly or rainy days.

Safety and Security in New York

Although New York City is typically safe for visitors, it is nevertheless important to exercise care as in any large city:

Be vigilant: Keep an eye on your possessions, particularly in busy places. To stave against pickpockets, use money belts or crossbody bags.

Use Reputable Transportation: Rely only on well-known, authorized taxi services, such as Uber or Lyft. Steer clear of unregistered or unauthorized cars.

Know Emergency Numbers: For instant help, get familiar with the local emergency numbers, including 911. There is a significant police presence in New York City, and assistance is always accessible.

Keep to Well-Lit Areas: When nighttime city exploration, stay on the city's busiest, well-lit streets. Avoid taking shortcuts via isolated or dark locations.

Avoid Street Solicitors: Be wary of persons selling things on the sidewalk or in the street. Refuse politely and continue going.

Navigating Public Transportation

The huge and effective public transit network in New York City makes getting around easy:

Subway: The quickest and most economical means of transportation inside the city is the subway. Learn the layout of the subway system, and think about getting a MetroCard for convenient access. Be mindful of service modifications, particularly on weekends and national holidays.

Buses: Buses are a useful addition to the subway system since they may carry you to places that are difficult to reach by rail. Bus routes are listed on the Metropolitan Transportation Authority (MTA) website, and bus stations are properly signposted.

Taxis: The whole city is well-served by yellow taxis. Make sure the taxi has a functional meter, and don't forget to leave the driver a tip. Several people also use ride-sharing services like Uber and Lyft.

Walking: Since New York City is a pedestrian-friendly area, exploring neighborhoods and famous sites on foot is sometimes the best option. For safety, crosswalks and pedestrian lights should be used.

Cycling: If you have cycling expertise, you may choose to hire a bike to explore the city's bike lanes and picturesque paths. Make sure you abide by the regulations of the road and wear a helmet.

Language and Cultural Tips

As a melting pot of languages and cultures, New York City, it is crucial to appreciate and be conscious of cultural diversity:

Language: Although English is the dominant language, you may hear several other languages being spoken all across the city. Language obstacles seldom arise since the majority of people and service providers are fluent in English.

Cultural Sensitivity: Respect various cultural customs and embrace the variety of the city. When meeting with individuals from different backgrounds, be kind and receptive.

Tipping: In New York City, tipping is traditional. It's customary to tip between 15% and 20% of the total cost at restaurants. For great service, you could also wish to provide tips to taxi drivers, tour guides, and hotel personnel.

Queuing: When waiting in lines or queues, remember that New Yorkers usually line up in a neat and organized form.

Greetings: A sincere "hello" or "thank you" may go a long way. The people of New York value civility and politeness.

By following these suggestions, you'll not only have a seamless and pleasurable trip to New York City during the holiday season but also help to ensure that everyone you come into contact with has a good and polite experience. You're now ready to enter the enchanted realm of a New York Christmas after finishing your preparations!

POST-CHRISTMAS ACTIVITIES

Your holiday-related New York Christmas trip need not come to an end. Chapter 10 of "A New York Christmas Odyssey: Your Seasonal Travel Guide" explores the fun possibilities for after-Christmas events, such as New Year's Eve parties, extending your stay, and the crucial measures for getting ready to go.

New Year's Eve Celebrations in the City

The Times Square ball drop is one of the most famous New Year's Eve events in New York City. The city that never sleeps offers a variety of ways to bring in the new year, including:

Times Square Ball Drop: Join the throng in Times Square for the traditional New Year's Eve event. Times Square Ball Drop. To have a good place to see the ball drop at midnight, go there early in the day. Expect lengthy lines, security inspections, and restricted access to the bathrooms.

New Year's Eve Parties: Expensive New Year's Eve parties and galas are held at several hotels, eateries, and clubs across the city. Gourmet meals, live entertainment, and champagne toasts at midnight are frequent features of these occasions. Make reservations as soon as possible since they book up rapidly.

Fireworks: Enjoy a spectacular fireworks show above the East River. For the greatest vistas, go to Brooklyn or Queens. Williamsburg and the Brooklyn Bridge provide beautiful backgrounds for ringing in the new year.

Dinner Cruises: On a New Year's Eve dinner cruise, you may toast the new year while dining on a fine meal and cruising the city's waterways. Live entertainment and excellent views of the pyrotechnics are often included with these trips.

Central Park Midnight Run: Take part in the annual Central Park Midnight Run if you want a more active celebration. All abilities are invited to participate in this four-mile race, which starts at midnight. It's a distinctive way to start the new year.

Extending Your Stay in New York

There are plenty of things to do in the city if you want to remain into the new year since you fell in love with the festive spirit:

Explore Cultural Institutions: The world-renowned museums, theaters, and galleries in New York are worth seeing. Spend your days touring the MoMA, the Metropolitan Museum of Art, Broadway plays, and other cultural attractions.

Winter Sports: Take advantage of the colder weather by visiting ice skating rinks like Bryant Park or Wollman Rink in Central Park. In close-by resorts, you may even give skiing or snowboarding a try.

Indoor Attractions: Explore the city's interior attractions, including the 9/11

Memorial & Museum, the Empire State Building, and the One World Observatory.

Food & Dining: Visit the famous restaurants in the city to sample a variety of cuisines as you continue your gastronomic exploration. New York provides a wide range of eating alternatives, from Michelin-starred restaurants to little neighborhood cafes.

Shopping: Explore the city's renowned retail areas, such as Fifth Avenue, SoHo, and the Lower East Side, and take advantage of the post-holiday bargains.

Preparing for Departure

Here are some crucial things to ensure a pleasant exit when your New York Christmas vacation draws to an end:

Review Your Itinerary: Double-check your trip itinerary, including the dates and hours of your flights or trains as well as your means of transportation to the airport or station. Ensure you have your boarding tickets, passport, or other identification papers before you leave.

Pack & Organize: Organize and pack your belongings: Start packing them up well before you go. If necessary, use the baggage storage at your hotel, and make sure you haven't forgotten anything in your room.

Settle Bills: Take care of any unpaid hotel bills, including those related to room rates, minibar costs, and restaurant tabs. Verify that any extra costs have been correctly invoiced.

Transportation: Make arrangements for transportation to the airport or train station. Public transportation, airport shuttles, ride-sharing services, and taxis are available options. Remember to account for anticipated traffic delays as well as travel time.

Currency Exchange: At the airport or nearby currency exchange offices, you could think about converting any extra U.S. dollars you may have into your own currency.

Thank You and Feedback: If you had a good time, think about writing the hotel employees a message of appreciation and sharing your thoughts on your stay. This could enhance subsequent visits.

Making the most of your time in New York City and planning your departure with these post-Christmas activities in mind can help you have a seamless and enjoyable holiday experience. Whether you're enjoying a peaceful moment in Central Park or watching the ball drop in Times Square, New York will leave you with priceless memories that you'll love forever. Goodbye to the city that never sleeps and till we meet again!

CONCLUSION

We hope that "New York Christmas Guide: Your Seasonal Travel Guide" has been your dependable travel companion, enhancing your experience and assisting you in making the most of this magnificent voyage as your Christmas adventure comes to an end. This tour has covered the charming customs, well-known sights, and undiscovered attractions that make Christmas in New York a really unique experience.

During your stay, New York City surely spun a tapestry of amazing memories, from the glittering lights of Rockefeller Center to the charming Christmas markets, from the comfortable cafés selling hot chocolate to the thrill of New Year's Eve festivities.

We've helped you with the planning process, given insights into the must-see locations, given advice on eating and cultural events, and even suggested ways to prolong your stay and go without a hitch. Our goal has been to make your experience celebrating Christmas in New York as easy, pleasurable, and memorable as possible.

You've probably experienced the friendliness and variety of the city's residents along the way. You've had the chance to immerse yourself in its rich tapestry of people by embracing New York's variety, which is a lively mosaic of cultures, languages, and customs.

Remember the happy times, the mouthwatering flavors, and the laughter you enjoyed with loved ones as you think back on your time spent in the city. These experiences will always be a part of your New York Christmas Odyssey, whether you stared at the holiday lights, yelled at the top of your lungs at a Broadway performance, or just enjoyed the thrill of a New York winter.

We want you to take a little bit of New York with you when you go home. All who come are inspired by the city's resiliency, innovation, and unlimited vitality. The Christmas season is a time for warmth, giving, and the pursuit of joy.

May your New York Christmas journey serve as a reminder that this world is full of magic.
Last but not least, keep in mind that New York City will always be waiting to welcome you back, whether it be for Christmas or any other time of the year. There are constantly fresh experiences waiting to be found thanks to the city's vivacious character.

You will always have a particular place in your heart for New York City, from the sparkling lights of the Christmas tree at Rockefeller Center to the busy streets of Manhattan and the tranquility of Central Park in the winter. So may your holiday season be full of wonder, love, and the enchantment of a New York Christmas until you return to the city that never sleeps. Happy Christmas and safe travels!

APPENDICES

In this last portion of "New York Christmas Guide: Your Seasonal Travel Guide," we provide you useful appendices to complement your trip to New York for the holidays. To make it simple for you to organize your days in the city, these tools contain helpful contacts and information, a thorough packing checklist, and example itineraries.

Useful Contacts and Resources

It's crucial to have access to vital connections and services while you're in New York City. The following list of helpful people and places might help you during your visit:

Emergency Services:

- Call 911 for police, fire, and medical emergencies.

Tourist Information:

- Visit NYC & Company's official website at www.nycgo.com.

- Visitor Information Centers in NYC: www.nycgo.com/visitorcenters

Transportation:

- MTA: www.mta.info Metropolitan Transportation Authority
- Airports and bus terminals are managed by the Port Authority of New York and New Jersey (www.panynj.gov).

Embassies and Consulates:

- Healthcare Services: travel.state.gov U.S. Department of State - List of Foreign Embassies and Consulates

Healthcare Services:

- Hospitals and medical facilities: Ask your lodging about local medical centers.

Weather Information:

- National Weather Service: www.weather.gov

Currency Exchange:

Locations for Currency Exchange: There are several banks and currency exchange offices spread all around the city.

Language Assistance:

- Numerous lodging establishments and companies provide multilingual help.

Packing Checklist

Use this packing list as a guide to make sure you have everything you need for your New York Christmas adventure:

Clothing:

- Winter coat or jacket
- Sweaters or fleeces
- Thermal undergarments
- Warm hats and scarves
- Gloves or mittens
- Waterproof and insulated boots
- Comfortable walking shoes
- Socks (thermal if possible)
- Comfortable, layered clothing

Travel Documents:

- Passport or ID
- Visa (if required)
- Travel insurance documents
- Flight/train tickets
- Hotel reservations
- Itinerary

Miscellaneous:

- Travel-sized laundry detergent
- Umbrella
- Reusable water bottle
- Ziplock bags (for snacks or toiletries)
- Earplugs and sleep mask (for light sleepers)
- Travel pillow
- Entertainment (books, e-reader, or games)
- Snacks and reusable shopping bag

Sample Itineraries

We have offered two example itineraries that appeal to various interests and tastes to assist you in organizing your days in New York City. You are allowed to alter them to reflect your own preferences and considerations.

Sample Itinerary 1: *Holiday Magic and Culture*

Note that the emphasis of this itinerary is on cultural and tourist destinations with a Christmas theme.

Day 1:

- ***Morning***: Visit the Rockefeller Center to view the Christmas tree and go skating.
- ***Afternoon***: Examine Fifth Avenue's Christmas window decorations.
- ***Evening***: Attend the Radio City Christmas Spectacular.

Day 2:

- ***Morning***: Enjoy a leisurely breakfast at a nearby café.
- ***Afternoon***: View the seasonal exhibits at the Metropolitan Museum of Art.
- ***Evening***: See "The Nutcracker" perform at Lincoln Center.

Day 3:

- ***Morning***: Go on a walking tour of several old churches to see how they celebrate Christmas.

- ***Afternoon***: Visit seasonal markets like Union Square seasonal Market to find one-of-a-kind presents.
- ***Evening***: Participate in a Central Park carol singing.

Sample Itinerary 2: *Outdoor Adventure & Exploration*

Note: The emphasis of this program is on neighborhood exploration and outdoor activities.

Day 1:

- ***Morning***: Take a stroll across Central Park.
- ***Afternoon***: Take a tour of Brooklyn's neighborhoods, including DUMBO and Williamsburg.
- ***Evening***: Enjoy supper at a Brooklyn waterfront restaurant.

Day 2:

- ***Morning***: Visit Ellis Island and the Statue of Liberty.

- ***Afternoon***: Enjoy the scenery by riding the Staten Island Ferry and strolling around Battery Park.
- ***Evening***: Go back to Manhattan to see a Broadway performance.

Day 3:

- ***Morning***: Go Ice Skating ⛸ in Central Park's Wollman Rink.
- ***Afternoon***: Explore Chelsea Market and the High Line Park.
- ***Evening***: Attend a rooftop party or take in Times Square's New Year's Eve festivities.

You're prepared to go off on your New York Christmas Adventure with the help of these helpful contacts, a thorough packing list, and example itineraries. Your vacation in the "city that never sleeps" is sure to be a wonderful and rewarding one, whether you decide to take part in Christmas enchantment, explore the city's neighborhoods, or do both at once. Happy Christmas and safe travels!